DOING Time

HOW TO BE
FREE IN YOUR
MARRIAGE

MERI HORTON

DOING TIME
How to Be Free in Your Marriage

merihorton@comcast.net

ISBN 978-1-943342-26-6

Published by: Destined To Publish | Flossmoor, Illinois
www.DestinedToPublish.com

DEDICATION

In memory of Pastor Karen Jackson:
You were an inspirational and supportive figure in my life. You were my personal intercessor. I loved your commitment to prayer, faith, obedience, and personal holiness. You discern the heart of God and war in heaven on behalf of others. Everyone needs a person like you in their life. I will forever cherish all the encouragement and love you showed me. Gone but never forgotten.

To my daughters:
Melanie Smith
Clarissa Horton
Angelica Horton

To my grandchildren:
Alliyah Bey
Alijay Bey

ABOUT US

Charles and Meri Horton, founders of Mission Possible Institute, have coached married and engaged couples for over 15 years. They are passionate about helping couples achieve successful marriages and watching their families prosper. As certified facilitators in Saving Your Marriage Before It Starts (SYMBIS) assessments, the Hortons work with engaged couples before they get married to help prepare them for lifelong love.

They are certified in Marriage on the Rock counseling to help couples succeed in a thriving and passionate marriage, and they have accredited Mental Health Coaches through Light University.

The Hortons have extensive experience in:

- couples coaching,
- family coaching,
- one-on-one coaching,
- webinars, and
- workshops.

Charles and his wife Meri married for 30 years and are still romantically in love. They are the proud parents of three children and two grandchildren.

Over 90% of my time counseling is spent with couples dealing with and recovering from infidelity. I have found that the path to recovery is very narrow, and establishing hope in both marriage partners can be very difficult. However, since I believe it is my job to help couples stay on the path by mapping out a plan and providing encouragement to continue, couples soon learn that the impossible can become possible.

I look forward to helping you soon.

Telephone number: (855) 927-3977

ACKNOWLEDGMENTS

I want to express my appreciation to the excellent team at Destined to Publish for their vision and heart to see this book come into being. I am forever grateful. I also want to thank my husband, Charles Horton, for his endless expression of love for our children and me. I love you and thank you for allowing me to express myself freely in sharing all that God has placed inside of me.

DION CAMPBELL

I often marvel at knowing that God's original intention for implementing the Kingdom of God was not the church but a man and a woman. The institution of marriage has been and will always be a priority in God's heart.

In this modern day and age, we see a deliberate attack on this sacred institution that destabilizes the nation's heart—the foundation of marriage matters. Fortunately for us, God has mandated Meri Horton to write and share her experiences to protect what is essential to Him . . . our marriages!

My wife and I have watched the hand of God move mightily upon Meri Horton as she and her husband, Charles, have been faithful to minister effective marriage practices to the Body of Christ. We are fortunate to have received Meri's insight and pour, contributing to our 30 years of marriage success. Watching Meri increase in wisdom and grace, knowledge, and faith has been a joy. Her expertise is needed in establishing modern-day relationships.

Trust me, what you have in your hand is not just a book of theories based on wishful thinking. This easy-to-read compilation is a bonafide relationship masterpiece that provides step-by-step instructions on how to build a successful marriage.

Meri has pivoted powerfully on proven principles and workable solutions developed in her personal life and successful marriage to Charles. That divinely ordered reality, combined with decades of strategies learned by building thousands of marriages through one-on-one sessions and numerous seminars, makes this a robust and panoramic resource.

Meri, you have penned a beautiful and professionally written work that gives us a glimpse into God's heart for his people by providing us with a clear pathway to life in the Kingdom. This work is truly a labor of love. Thank you, Meri!

Dion Campbell

Chief Of Police | Michigan City, Indiana
Sharpening Stone International Apostolic Team
Certified Jimmy Evans Marriage on the Rock Instructor

CONTENTS

INTRODUCTION

A great marriage is possible!

I am sitting on the patio in Ocho Rios, Jamaica, celebrating our 30th wedding anniversary. As I reflect on my life and how "we could have stayed together simply for the sake of not getting divorced,"? (*Doing time*).

I see couples, seemingly happy, walking on the beach. I can't help but wonder how many are actually enjoying themselves, or are they simply going through the motions (doing time) and not happy—not dealing with issues? These issues lie dormant in the soul.

I am Meri Horton, a wife of 30 years, a mother of three beautiful daughters, and an Abuela of two. I was doing time. I was simply going through the motions of living. If you looked at me from the outside, you would think I had it together. The pain on the inside was unbearable. The anxiety and fear of getting a divorce tormented me. I was willing to endure the pain so I did not have to deal with the shame. You see, this is my second marriage. I was dealing with pain, rejection, and infidelity. I was the common denominator! I was repeating the same mistakes I had made in my first relationship. I somehow felt attracted to and comfortable on this path. Do you or someone you know repeat the same mistakes in relationships? This book will walk you through similar situations and teach you how to break that cycle.

I understand not wanting to deal with the issue and the drama that comes with it very well. I am glad that instead, we allowed God to work in us. I am so happy that we stayed together and not only stayed together but had a very good marriage. It wasn't easy, but it was worth it.

Many are afraid and unable to function in their marriages because they cannot get past the pain and embarrassment in their lives. Have you experienced any of the following?

- Hurt
- Strife
- Envy
- Outrage
- Hatred
- Jealousy
- Anger
- Bitterness
- Resentment
- Suspicion

You are not alone!

Doing Time will help you encounter God's Word and learn from your mistakes to apply God's Word to your marriage if you want God's best. This book is not a theory, but you will see the Word of God made flesh in my marriage. This book will provide tools and basic examples of applying God's Word to your marriage. Fasten your seat belt. You are getting ready to ride through my life and the lives of women like me. I pray that this book will reveal life-giving principles for developing healthy, loving marriages and set you free from the bondage of shame and unforgiveness.

This book is intended to help you resist the temptation to run away from your marriage.

The book you are holding will change your relationship. I can confidently say this, not because I wrote it, but because I know what it has done for me. You will face difficult obstacles and will overcome them. The disciples of Jesus witnessed many miracles, from raising the dead to deadly storms right before their eyes, and so will you. I declare that you will notice your marriage being raised from the dead as you go through the storm. You will see the Word of God in 3D, increasing your faith.

This is quite possibly the most transparent book you will encounter in your life.

Do you want to stop the divorce proceedings? If you are ready for a change, need to be encouraged, and have lost faith in your marriage, you have picked up the right book.

No two marriages are the same, but God knows you and your spouse. If you apply the Word of God to your marriage, you will have a great marriage.

Don't let the enemy lure you into his ugly jaws. He is cunning.

Do not let pride hold you back. Incorporate prayer and reading time so you can recognize his traps. Please note—infidelity alone is not deadly, but what is deadly is not getting to the core of the problem. This book reveals my pain and chronicles how I dealt with it.

Grow in faith, and you will enjoy your marriage. Be free in Jesus's name!

The Spirit of God spoke to me and said that many would be healed and freed by reading this book and burned this in my heart.

I believe that as you read this book, God will teach you personally. As he does, you will receive great freedom in your marriage. I desire that God awaken you to your proper condition.

Pride will keep you from acknowledging your condition because pride masks your heart's exact condition—your pain.

You can put this book down if you think it is about bashing men.

You're mistaken if you think this book is about me being a victim.

I have a pure heart for marriages because I have dealt with my pain, anger, and unforgiveness. I am not walking around as a victim.

I pray that God will open the eyes of your understanding so you can see the actual condition of your heart.

You have a choice to make!

"Doing time" is defined as staying married for being married, but you are miserable. . simply going through the motions of living.

Don't brag about being together for twenty years if you've been crying for nineteen! God wants healthy people, not just the preservation of marriage. Christ died to save souls, not institutions.

CHAPTER 1

BUSTED

The day our lives changed

Sometimes life isn't what you expect it or plan it to be. As humans, we sometimes imagine that life will turn out a certain way and reality has a way of waking us up. Growth is uncomfortable, but it benefits us. It certainly does not feel good when it happens, but it is much easier if you trust the process.

Commitment is not enjoyed by many in our society. Our society emphasizes individual rights and personal freedom. The very thought of giving these up scares most couples. Commitment to another person makes many people feel trapped.

But can you have a good marriage and remain unwilling to change? You don't give up all your freedoms or choices, but it does mean your commitment to the relationship is more significant than your rights.

The day our lives changed, the unthinkable happened. The waves of reality were rapidly crashing into my life, and it was like a boat filling up with water before it started to sink. Early in our marriage, I noticed that my husband was acting differently. For instance, there was no eye contact, and things didn't add up. He always had an innocent explanation but was just becoming very inconsistent. I did not want to say anything and disturb the peace. I wanted to be mistaken and not face the fact that something was wrong.

When his infidelity was exposed, I was devastated. I realized everything was not what I thought. We were both living a lie. My "happily ever after" had been tarnished by the discovery of my husband's unfaithfulness. We had become born-again believers in 1991. We were both active in the ministry. We attended church every Wednesday and Sunday. But then facts started to surface!

It was spring, a gloomy day. It rained on and off all day. I was at home watching television with my two youngest daughters. My husband told me he was spending the evening with his brother. Something didn't quite settle in my spirit, man. I thought I was tripping, so I did not say anything. Soon after, I got a call from a young lady stating she had been seeing my husband, and she felt I should know... As I sat in my family room, the pain, fear, and anxiety I felt were unbearable. I envisioned myself raising my girls as a single mother once again. I already had a daughter from my first marriage and had raised her as a single mom. I did not want to do it again. I did not sign up for this! My mind was flooded with all kinds of thoughts. I FELT STUPID when I was going through this period; how could I let this happen again? What will the family think? I did not want him to be labeled as a "cheater."

I felt not good enough! I questioned myself; was I pretty enough, a good cook, a good housekeeper, a good wife, a good lover, a good mother, a good friend? I had let my guard down and looked at what had happened. I thought I had met someone who would heal and protect me. Not a person who would hurt me like in every other relationship I'd had. I thought this was different!

I thought to myself, how do I get out of this? I'm scared, but I can't allow him to see me like this. How can I discuss this with anyone? I felt lonely and afraid of what else would come out.

As he walked through the door. I let him have it. I immediately confronted him. I started asking all types of questions. I did not bother to ask him if it was true. I was angry and hurt, and I wanted him to feel the same way or worse. His first instinct was to deny it all.

I did not know how to react to him denying everything. I instantly found myself responding to specific triggers and situations from past relationships.

I assumed his telling me the truth would be a relief for him (a tremendous load off his shoulders), now that it was out in the open— "Whew! It's finally over. I can move on." But things did not go quite that way.

I assume he felt scared I would leave him if he told me the truth. I sure did not demonstrate by my actions that I was open to forgiveness.

He was talking as little as could be expected - just everything he believed he needed to say, and that's it.

I wondered why it was so hard for him to talk about it. My husband did not want to keep discussing it all of the time. To him, it was finished and in the past, and he might want to let it be because he would rather not hurt me again. He was protecting my feelings. He would have preferred not to harm me any further.

Meanwhile, I had an intense need to know what had happened, and I did not want or need any more surprises.

I understand this is reasonable because, essentially, no one—on any issue—needs to reveal things they realize will intentionally provoke awful responses. Human survival generally relies on avoiding potential loss: marriage, kids, home, finances, social standing, etc. There are additional explanations behind avoiding undertaking these difficult conversations, which we will examine later in the book.

As the days passed, I ran on empty and cared very little about anything. I put no effort into making my marriage work. I had no energy and no hope to proceed.

I did not fight for myself. I was destroying him, and I was killing us. That didn't go too well, as you will see as you continue reading.

Self-Reflection:

Are you in survival mode?

1. Are you just trying to get through the day?

2. Do you feel like you will never dig yourself out of your hole?

3. Do you barely have the energy to answer the phone, return calls, or meet urgent deadlines? Do you make excuses for missing them?

4. Is the stress overwhelming? Your sleep is disrupted, your breathing feels odd, your heart beats erratically, and you can't think straight. Do you tell yourself to calm down, but it doesn't work?

5. Do you feel that there is no joy? Is your goal to avoid having a terrible day because having a great day isn't an option?

6. Is everything a reaction?

CHAPTER 2

MIDNIGHT EXPRESS

Run from it all

When you hear the expression "run," you most likely think of a teen escaping from a messed-up home, a father running from child support, or a thief fleeing from the police. A person in pain may also feel they are running to get away from the pain. Generally, the longing to run is filled with the hope of escaping a terrible situation or circumstance. Individuals who need to run are usually worried or discontent with their problems and frantically searching for an exit plan. Burnout is often the source of the desire to run away. Prolonged and excessive stress will drain you and cause you to make emotional decisions.

No two people are alike, so I am not saying that you should do things exactly the way I did. What I am saying is that you can learn from some of my mistakes. I failed to take time for myself.

All I did every day was focus on what my husband was doing, scared of what would happen next. I was mentally exhausted. It consumed my life. I woke up every morning fretting over what would, who would call me, who would say what. Could I handle what the day was going to bring? I decided to expect the worst, so I would not be disappointed.

I learned early on that fulfilling your responsibilities to others is easier when you are in suitable physical, mental, and emotional health. I am not saying that you should neglect your marriage and children. I am saying that self-care is vital.

One day I woke up and said to myself, and I probably said it out loud, "I can't handle this! I want the pain to go away."

My heart was shattered. I had nightmares every night. I woke up often during the night. When I did sleep, I still woke up irritable, feeling like I had not slept. I would go to work every day, but I could not focus. My mind was clouded. I made many errors and was very impatient with my customers.

Feeling nervous, restless, and tense was my norm.

I began to wonder what this would be like for the rest of my life. Is this what married life is like? Couples are miserable but stay together to say they are married.

One day, I woke up with this fantastic idea and knew what I would do. I was going to stop the pain. I was leaving. I would pack my stuff and leave at night when he was not around. I would take a leave of absence from my job and move to Puerto Rico for several months. A different place with different people would surely help. At least it would stop me from thinking about all my problems and clear my head.

I had many conversations with myself.

I had to ask myself *why* I was running away. I asked myself, *is simply running away from this situation going to solve the problem? What are the pros and cons of running away?* I asked myself these questions over and over again in my head. If I have to be honest, I answered them differently every time, depending upon how I felt at the moment. When I was in the presence of God, I felt safe and like there was nothing I could not do. I felt like Peter; I could walk on water.

I knew I had to make a decision. I decided to stay and work it out. I decided that neither the circumstances of his actions nor my emotions would dictate my actions. I admit I was scared and questioned if this was God's best for me.

If your life is at risk, maybe leaving is the best option. Everyone needs to know that there are alternatives to running away. Running away is not your only option.

I admit that I initially did not speak to anyone who could help me with my marriage. I talked to many people but shared things that painted him badly. I shared information out of my pain.

I was not talking to anyone that could help me resolve our problems. After talking to many people and getting tired of talking, I felt "in my head." I was feeling anxious and exhausted. I appreciated the people who spent countless hours listening to me and trying to help the best they could, but I was talking to the wrong people. I wanted my marriage. I wanted to be happy, and if my current situation was what marriage felt like, I did not want to be married. Deep down inside, I did want to stay married. I loved my husband, but I did not like him. I spoke to some women in the church, but they were just as unhappy, or more so than I was. They were "doing time" as if everything was fine. *God, forbid we get a divorce and make the church look bad. Just stay married. You will get used to it,* is what they advised. I went straight to the pastor and his wife and sought help. I knew if we were going to get past this, we needed help fast. I just knew that talking to the pastor would fix everything right away. He would advise and give us some scriptures, and we would live happily ever after...

Self-Reflection:

1. Do you want to stay married?

2. Do you want to stop the pain?

3. Are you tired of talking and feeling hopeless?

4. Is running away from this situation going to solve the problem?

\
\
\

5. Do you want to stay married to say you are married?

\
\
\

CHAPTER 3

CONTROL CENTER

Pros and Cons of Christian Marriage Counseling

The control room is the nerve center of most modern prisons and detention centers. In this room, the officer's job is to monitor prison traffic and ensure that prisoners are where they should be.

Christian marriage mentoring may mean various things to various individuals; however, it generally implies getting marriage mentoring from the perspective of religion. Strict anecdotes, sacred texts, and beliefs are utilized to move toward the issues the married couple is having and, ideally, resolve them so they can have a long and blissful life together.

On my way to our meeting with Pastor, I was so angry that I yelled at a stop sign. As I walked into Pastor's office, I told myself, *When I leave this meeting, I will go from surviving to striving!*

Our pastor was our marriage counselor. We went for advice, to discuss our marital issues, and more.

I could not wait for our first meeting with our pastor. I was prepared to tell my pastor every detail, and I just knew he would tell my husband off, and I would leave there feeling accomplished.

Instead, I left there with an assignment to read First Corinthians 13, the love chapter. *Are you kidding me? You want me to walk in love? Why are you even talking to me about walking in love? We wouldn't be here if my husband were walking in love! Please do not make this about me.* I thought it would be best to talk to him and teach him to be a man of God and a husband. Imagine my face when he didn't want to hear all the details or how I felt. I thought to myself, the *pastor is a chauvinist!* I would not dare say it to him; I had too much respect for him. I had no idea it would turn out this way.

I was shocked, hurt, offended, disinterested, and hopeless. It was a long meeting! We discussed what the Bible said about marriage, commitment, and expectations. We were not taught how to handle conflict, solve problems, or set priorities in marriage. I had no idea how to fight. You see, I knew how to fight the way the world fought. So, when I did not get quick results, I reverted to my old ways. I was told what my role was and what his role was, but I did not know how to apply it in this new Christian walk.

All I could feel was my heartbreak. I felt Pastor was making excuses for my husband. I felt lightheaded, and there was a sudden feeling of everything spiraling out of control. I was having an anxiety attack. I was so embarrassed! I felt like this weak-crazy woman. When looking, I recall that the fearfulness, overwhelming hopelessness, and racing heart did not end at this meeting. Every decision I made was based on fear.

When I looked at my future, I did not see happiness. I felt ugly, not good enough. I refused to take pictures because I did not want to remember these moments. I was afraid people would see the pain in my eyes and the stress on my face, which aged me. On our way home, he turned around, and as soon as our eyes met, I thought, *He did not intend to hurt me.* Then my next thought was, *I don't care. I can't trust him. I can't let my guard down; I will never love him again as I did. I can't be hurt like this again.* It weighed heavy on my soul.

You might think I'm crazy, but I am just being transparent and vulnerable. How could I quit being angry after my significant other engaged in extramarital relations? We were attempting to resolve it. However, I couldn't relinquish the resentment which drove him away. I needed to hurt him as he broke me; however, I would rather not lose him. What to do? **I felt conflicted and confused. I did NOT want to love him!**

I made a lot of bad choices, and I reacted very carnally. Looking back, I can now see I added to the problem.

Charles and I battled with allowing God to work on us individually that summer. I started to struggle with who I was and who he was. I thought I would never be truly happy in my marriage again. I let those thoughts get into my head and heart and internalized them. As much as I tried not to, I loved him, but I didn't want to get my hopes up, nor did I know if he would ever be the right one for me.

There were red flags about each other that we ignored from the very beginning. I foolishly thought they would disappear or outgrow them if we pretended not to see them.

Feeling furious is a normal reaction to the betrayal. He broke my trust. I did not know how to deal with my emotions. You see, God gave us feelings. They are a gift from God, but how we respond to those emotions counts. I did not know how to react to them, so I suppressed them.

As you read, you will see that I learned why my pastor addressed it the way he did. But at the moment, all I could hear was what he said to me.

Follow your pastor's direction as long as their leadership is consistent with scripture. If you disagree, pray for them instead of criticizing and talking negatively. Let God deal with it. The Holy Spirit can do a much better job than we can. I thought no more secrets; everything was out in the open.

Self-Reflection:

1. Are you feeling anxious about the situation?

2. Do you feel heard?

3. Do you feel conflicted and confused?

4. Do you feel like you are on an emotional roller coaster?

5. Are you willing to walk the process out?

CHAPTER 4

POTTING

Lies and denial

Potting - prison slang for throwing or dumping a bucket of excrement on a correctional officer.

His side of the story

As the husband, I was living a lie, but I was present every time the church doors opened, rain or shine.

I was even working in ministry, and tonight was Wednesday night Bible study.

I vividly remember this Wednesday. I was in my bedroom watching pornography and heard my wife open the door. I quickly took the videotape out of the VCR and hid it in my drawer. I greeted my wife and kids as if nothing was wrong...I was addicted.

I quickly left for Bible Study. My wife and kids stayed home.

When I arrived, the church secretary ran to me, saying my wife was on the phone.

I never imagined what was going on. I said, "Hello," and my wife was screaming on the other end of the phone. I could barely understand what she was saying, and then I heard her say that she had found the porn tapes and my stash of adult magazines.

All I could think about was, how much does she know? At that moment, I wasn't worried about my marriage, children, or relationship with God—I WAS CAUGHT!

I was selfish, I know, not thinking about the impact of my actions on everyone involved or my future. The days ahead were hard, but one of the men at the church started mentoring me. He prayed with me, and we would read the Word. This was precisely what I needed: prayer, accountability, and hope. As I looked at my wife and girls and saw the pain, I prayed to be the best husband and father I could be.

I only knew one way! It was to cry out to God. I stayed on my knees and cried out for the mercy of God. I did not go through a twelve-step program, but I now understand the confession of being an addict. An addict is only one look or thought away from relapse. I have to pray and kill my flesh daily, so the addiction does not win.

You have to ask God to reveal the root of the problem. The Bible talks about being drawn away by your lust and enticed in the first chapter of James. So, when it comes to porn addiction, don't try to hide it. Confess it to God first, then others affected, for complete forgiveness and healing. The Bible reminds us to flee from sin. I learned that it was not worth it. I let down God, my wife, my family, and myself. Getting out of this wasn't easy, but God brought me through in his grace and mercy. Intercession is vital and needed. God does not want us to bear our burdens alone.

***

As the wife, I remember it like yesterday: Wednesday was a rainy and gloomy day.

I rushed into the house with two young toddlers to prepare for the evening. I decided not to attend Bible study and stayed home. As I was going about the evening, I went into my husband's dresser to put his clothes away and found pornographic videos. I then went looking for what else I could find. In the garage were more videos and adult magazines. Without even thinking, I ran to the phone and called the church. When he got on the phone, I went off! I was going to tell the pastor and anyone else that would listen. I wanted him to feel the pain and embarrassment. *Who is this man? Do I know him?* This resulted in my insecure feelings and low self-esteem. I did not feel good enough. I had been betrayed.

I would constantly be disrespectful; I had lost all respect for him. I was hurting emotionally, spiritually, and physically. I was in pain! I thought to myself, *What's next? Is there more I don't know about this man?*

Self-Reflection:

1. Do you believe there are always two sides to every story?

2. Do you feel others are trying to manipulate you?

3. Are you playing the role of the hero, and naturally, the other party is the villain?

4. Is another party out to get you?

25

CHAPTER 5

PRISON GUARDS (MINISTERS)

Stop the bleeding & ensure accountability

I walked into the minister's office in desperation. I boldly stated, "I need help letting go of the pain. I need help learning how to walk in forgiveness. When I think I am moving forward, I take two steps backward. Was there something leading up to this that I missed? Someone, please help me."

I had many questions but was unsure if I was ready for the answers. I wanted to wake up and realize it was just a bad dream. "How will I learn how to trust again? Should I let my guard down? Is this healthy? Someone help me! I am scared! How can I believe again? Why should I forgive him? I don't think he understands what he did and its impact on my life. Please help me!"

As I look back, all our conversations turned into arguments. You could imagine how it worsened if we had problems communicating before the affair. I became manipulative. I turned every argument into his fault. In my mind, I thought I was the innocent one! I used emotional blackmail as a weapon. Emotional manipulation is something I was good at. It was very subtle and harmless at times, but it was very damaging in reality. I used his weaknesses against him. I told myself he would have to deal with my behavior. The blame games—"It couldn't possibly be my fault! You were the blatantly unfaithful one."

I refused to look in the mirror because I had decided that I was right and he was wrong. Please note that I am not saying that what he did was not bad. I am being honest about my behavior. Two wrongs do not make a right. If you want Godly results, you must do it in God's way. When God deals with my marriage, he talks to me about me.

Self-Reflection:

1. Have you ever asked yourself these questions:

2. How will I learn how to trust again?

3. Will I ever believe in true love again?

4. Will I be able to let my guard down?

____

____

____

____

5. Have you ever felt scared to be vulnerable?

____

____

____

____

When I look at them, will I see what God's Word says about my spouse?

Meditate on that.......

As I sat with the minister at the church and attempted to establish a plan, the minister explained that forgiveness is a gift to me, and we discussed the benefits and reasons behind forgiveness. You see, unforgiveness will weigh you down. I felt like I had a ton of bricks around my neck.

Sitting there, I wondered whether I was ready for a courageous conversation. Suddenly, big drops of sweat started rolling down my face; I felt my jaw tightening. Is asking a lot of questions a good thing? I felt like I was going to have an anxiety attack.

The minister interrupted my thoughts. He said, "Meri, write down your thoughts to communicate your truth; how are you starting your conversation? How are you sharing, so they get heard? You need a solid foundation system; a framework example avoids triggers. What to do when they pop up? They will come up, but you can control them when they do. What is causing the trigger? How do you respond to them? Watch your tone of voice and body language."

We discussed what I call verbal beat-up. When you verbally abuse your spouse and feel justified because they hurt you. The attitude of "I want you to feel what I feel." The "I am going to make you suffer" tactics. "I will put you through hell and justify the behavior." I now understand why they say, "hurt people, hurt people." I remember we stayed up all night arguing and getting up early to work after a sleepless night. I would ask him questions, expecting him to answer every question, no matter how tired he was. No answer was good enough. Looking back, I did not realize or probably even care if we lost sleep and could not function correctly throughout the day at work. He was suffering a physical and mental breakdown. Losing sleep affects jobs and relationships. The unfaithful spouse also suffers—the unfaithful deals with shame and exposure.

I remember waking up and thinking, *Today, I am calling our friends, family, and church family and telling them everything he has done, and I'm going to humiliate him.* I had checked out mentally and spiritually! I knew I had to decide to move forward, stay where we were at, or leave. I knew I wanted to be healed; I did not want to stay married for the sake of being married and miserable. I was not willing to become a product of my environment.

Why do we lie? Why do we put ourselves in predicaments that can cause us to stumble?

I ask myself whether I can handle the truth. Will all the details help or hurt me? I have a photographic memory, so I remember things in pictures. So, will all the details benefit me? I have heard many couples say they lie to protect their spouses. I can see that now, but I thought that was an excuse back then. My theory back then (no grace) was that you wouldn't have to lie if you did not put yourself in that predicament. Stop lying and start living. Getting counseling/therapy is my current stance.

I remember feeling like a failure of a failing family. I struggled to move beyond mental blocks.

You see, this was my second marriage. In my first marriage, I struggled with insecurity, rejection, and infidelity on his part. I never received healing. I thought getting a divorce and moving on to someone who loved me would improve everything. I thought he was the problem, and if I just found someone who would love me, I would be genuinely whole!

You see, my pain was so much deeper than that. My pain and rejection came from when I was a child. I was sexually abused as a child, so I married to get out of the house. I never received healing from that. I thought getting out of the situation was sufficient. I realize now that I have run from my past and have never dealt with the root of the problem. I don't want to continue to hurt.

At one point, I had a lightbulb moment; I was determined that my past would not control my future. But how would I accomplish that?

I had no idea the road to my recovery would be so difficult. I had so many regrets; there was a grieving process. My emotions were all over the place. One day I was okay. The next day or moment, I was not. I would catch my mind wondering how he could love me and do this to me; the next moment, I would think, *He is human. He is a new believer.* I was mentally exhausted. At times I felt hopeless, especially when I tried and failed.

DISCLAIMER: I am not telling you what and how to handle your issue; I am simply sharing my story, hoping God will use me.

As I sat there, listening to the minister, I thought I needed to start working on myself to make a clear decision. I knew it wouldn't be easy, but it was worth it. Are you happy, or are you "just doing time"?

I was hoping to leave inspired, and I was, for a moment.

Self-Reflection:

1. Can you recover from the hurt?

2. Are you willing to put in the work?

3. Are you open to healing?

4. What if you don't heal?

5. What are the benefits of recovery?

6. Does your spouse deserve to be forgiven?

7. What is your motivation?

____

____

____

____

____

You have to make up your mind and make a Godly decision. You have to have a clear sense.

CHAPTER 6

PSYCHOPATHY

Abnormal or violent behavior

Talking to the other person can go several ways. Sometimes, it splits apart a deceiving mate and their lover. Sometimes it misfires. It can draw a cheating spouse and another person closer together.

You never really know how a person is going to react. Specific individuals respond by withdrawing, others respond by retaliating, and some will attempt to stay away from the showdown.

What can go wrong? If the other individual knows private information concerning your relationship, that will add to the pain. Will your spouse take your side? Or will your spouse feel sorry for their lover? Will confronting the other person force your spouse to make a decision? In such situations, expecting your spouse to stay neutral is not realistic. There are many pros and cons you have to think about. Some can add salt to an existing wound.

The other woman/man can be demeaning and reinforce insecurities you may already have. You may find out something that may shock you. Ask yourself if this is going to hinder your relationship.

I wanted to confront the other woman.

Should I confront my spouse's mistress? This is a question you must ask yourself and meditate on before approaching them. Remember, you will face someone with little respect for your feelings.

What is your motive? Is it seeking information?

I perceived the other woman as a perpetrator.

I did not want to believe that it was my man's fault.

He has been tempted away. It was emotionally beneficial for me to think this way.

I can boldly confess I was not in my right mind. I can now see my immaturity. There was so much tension in our household. I felt different every day. Some days, I was good, and others, I was not. I felt hurt and unloved. I needed reassurance. He would attempt to pour his heart out to me, and I would be disrespectful by not allowing him to finish. I could not let my guard down and get hurt again. I told him I needed him to hear my heart to understand, so he could help me or know how to pray for me. *There is a pain deep in my soul. I am not sure the pain of betrayal will ever go away. Come close, listen to me.*

We were on different pages. He wanted me to get over it so we could continue with our lives, but I was afraid that if I got over it quickly, he would think it wasn't as bad as it was and continue hurting me. I was so hurt that when he assumed I was better after a few days passed without us discussing my thoughts or feelings, I went back into a rage. I thought to myself, *whom am I kidding?* I said, "I don't love you! I'm not too fond of anything about you." I wanted him to hurt so he wouldn't get away with it. I told him, "This is precisely what happens when you try to fix things yourself! Now, pray and believe God to heal me!" You see, when a woman feels unloved, she acts disruptively. When a man feels disrespected, he acts unloving, as we later learned from author Dr. Emerson Eggerich's teaching in *Love and Respect*. When needs are not met, we react negatively.

Self-Reflection:

1. Have you ever had a conflict where the issue was not the real issue?

2. How did you handle the conflict?

3. Do you know the root of the problem?

4. Do you have a strong desire for respect for your spouse?

5. Do you have a strong passion for love?

I understand why you would want to hurt the other individual for contributing so much hurt to your life. There are different ways to get closure.

There was a couple who truly loved each other. The man thought to himself, *how did we get here? We might not always see eye to eye, but how did we get here?* His spirit was deflated. He knew what he did was wrong. There was no way around it. He could not tell her all the details because he wanted to protect her. Giving all the pieces would only add to her pain, so he lied. He said he did not remember. He had to save her. Even in moments of anger, he had to protect her and the kids.

He had to defend himself at all costs. He messed this up, and he was going to fix it.

His wife came into the kitchen screaming at the top of her lungs. "And you are a treacherous scumbag who couldn't even be trusted to keep your marriage vows! You were willing to destroy our relationship and family for a piece. Your actions will affect the kids for the rest of their life. I hope it was worth it," she yelled as she stormed out of the room. After a long night, the conversation the following day was about her wanting to meet her.

She picked up the phone and dialed her number. Before she could finish saying hello, she started yelling, "This is his wife, so you know. He will never in this life leave me. I am his wife; that is something you will never be able to say. I will always be his priority. You will spend the holidays alone. You are a liar. You were living a lie. You will think about him more often than he ever thinks about you. You are a loser."

She asked the mistress, "Does being a mistress play a significant role in your self-esteem? Doesn't it make you feel bad about yourself? Are you okay being the *other woman*? Are you all right with this arrangement?" She did not wait or pause for her to answer. She said, "Godspeed!" and threw the phone at her husband. She asked him, "Do you love her?" as she braced herself for his answer.

Self-Reflection:

1. Is it worth contacting the other partner?

2. Do you know how the other individual is likely to respond?

3. How do you expect your spouse to answer?

4. Are you confronting the other individual to seek vengeance?

____

____

____

____

I strongly recommend considering the pros and cons of contacting the other person.

For example, what if you discover that your spouse is talking about you, adding more salt to the wound?

Will the conversation be beneficial? Can you handle all the facts? Why do you need to know? Is it helpful or hurtful?

Will this set you back or help you move forward?

Will it reveal crucial details?

Will it cause more drama?

An affair is a secret lie, so why would they be honest? You cannot take what the affair partner says at face value.

Be mindful before you decide if it's worth approaching the mistress. Exposing him destroys him and further complicates the situation.

So, assuming you are standing up to this individual to vent your anger, know that there are more valuable ways of achieving this.

You cannot determine how you are going to respond. It may infuriate you and end up doing something that puts you behind bars.

I remember a couple we worked with; the wife unexpectedly arrived home and heard her husband having sex. She ran out the door to the back of the house, threw nail polish all over the back door, and lit a match. She was attempting to stop his lover from leaving through the back door. She ran to the front of the house and entered the house when her husband stopped her. He called the police, and his wife was arrested.

 As the wife sat in jail, she felt betrayed. It felt like he was defending and protecting the mistress. She went through grief, frustration, disappointment, and lies. Yes, lies. She felt that there the whole relationship was a lie. How could they ever come back from that? You see, you never know how you are going to react. There are different approaches we can take. We know we must love each other whether or not we feel our partner deserves it.

You see, mistrust can confuse. How can we resist this downward spiral? How will we establish intimacy again?

All this drama was so embarrassing. There are other ways to get closure.

I told myself at some point, *let yourself open up and trust somebody... but wait just to get injured.* Do you know how difficult the sting of betrayal can be? I told myself, *try not to allow yourself to get hurt by lies. Safeguard yourself and try to see today!* Let's be clear: I knew I could not live this way if I would walk in God.

But wait, there's more...If you think you're ready, keep reading.

Self-Reflection:

1. Do you want to hurt the other individual for contributing so much hurt to your life?

2. Will confronting the other person force your spouse to make a decision?

3. Are you strongly considering the pros and cons of contacting the other person?

4. Are you confronting the other individual to look for vengeance?

CHAPTER 7

NOT A SCOOBY (I HAD NO CLUE)

Do the work! Nobody can do it for you!

I don't think we had any idea of what to do next.

My mind is swirling. I have no clue! I don't have the wildest idea of what to say or do. I am tired! I want this to end. Lord, please make this all go away.

Lord, you loved me when I was unlovable, but I don't know how to do that. I need a miracle. I do not want to walk this out. It might not surprise you to know that I was up all night. I was physically and mentally tired. I was so unsure what to do next. I had so many questions. How do I make the necessary changes to find, restore, and keep passionate love? I was familiar with this behavior; I had been through this before in my first marriage, but this time it was different. We were both going to church, supposedly living a Christian life, but my expectations differed. I liked being married, but I didn't want to be married just to say I was married. I wanted to enjoy my life. I prefer the traditional roles of husband and wife, and one of those roles is the husband being a protector, but at that point in my marriage, he was not fulfilling that role.

I had the opportunity to hear a young lady share her story at a Christian women's retreat. She stated:

> I recently discovered that my husband cheated on me with several ladies. He had several emotional affairs at work and church. This was not his first marriage, and he had a secret love child with another woman during his first marriage. His first wife had no clue about that, and I only found out when the child support agency sent a letter to our home. I also received a letter that he broke up with the other woman when she told him she was pregnant.

> She had an investigator follow him and figured out he had several women at a time. As I listened intensely, the fear went through my body. I wondered how someone could be so evil and heartless with no morals. I tried to figure out how I could cause him to acknowledge how his activities were killing our marriage. We have children, and I want to make things work for us. Wow, I understand making it work for the kids; however, what about *my* self-

esteem and self-respect? Random thoughts ran through my head. *What am I teaching my daughters by staying with him? It is not okay to be treated this way!*

I'm so hurt now, but it will be a long, hard road ahead if I stay in this marriage. Should I hire a darned good lawyer and find out my rights? And perhaps someday, I may find an outstanding, honest man with integrity and one I can fully trust. I was grieving. Will I ever recover? Only time will tell. I told myself, *you have choices. Use your boldness and creativity and make arrangements to go it all alone.*

I realized there is absolutely nothing you can do to make this man a less cold, heartless person. He is not worth you. Your relationships are telling you all that...loud and clear!

My friends would tell me, "If your man isn't willing to regard and cherish you enough to invest the energy and build a solid foundation, he isn't the person. This guy is a nightmare! He has cheated on you not just once but several times. What will make him change? I hate to say it, but you're just going to get hurt. You can't change him. You don't want to hear it, but it's the truth. He's cheated on you several times. Get away from him."

I nearly veered my car off the road when I burst into tears and yelled, is this how you want to live the rest of your married life? I was in a very dark place in my marriage. There was anger, resentment, and mistrust in my heart. Staying with an immoral man, a man you can't trust... will give you what? Nothing but a toxic relationship and a sinkhole under your heart, eventually.

I could not move past his past behavior of lying and cheating. Will this mistrust always punch holes in my heart?

Is he worth the time and effort? Especially when there is someone out there whom you could fully trust someday. A good, solid relationship should never have this type of worry you are experiencing. Maybe you should ask yourself why you are putting up with it. You won't change him. So, what do you need to do to change yourself?

I had a plan. I was going to start with the basics. *I will learn to have a ton of self-love and self-awareness about what makes me the happiest in life. I will work hard to reconnect with myself. I will choose what seems like the better course for myself and my girls. I will have a lot of bumps and humps to get over, but eventually, following the path of awareness will get me where I want to go and give me the happiness I deserve. I am young and have my whole life in front of me. It will be hard to make significant changes like this, but I deserve much more!*

Just when I thought I had decided to leave and move forward with my life, I woke up one day thinking, *Wait, I do want this marriage! Our marriage is worth it!* "Lord God," I prayed, "what does it take to get to him? When I think we have connected, he does or says something to prove he never understood what I said. It seems he cares more about his work [or sports or hobbies] than he does about me."

It should be no surprise that my emotions were all over the place. At that point, it appeared that I was determined to make this marriage work… come hell or high water. I was willing to do the job. I acknowledged that nobody could do it for me. I wanted us to honor our commitments, learn to apologize and forgive, and journey through life together.

For better or for worse…

Self-Reflection:

1. Do you want to honor your commitment and continue the journey together?

2. Do you enjoy being married?

3. Do you spend lots of time trying to figure your spouse out?

4. Do you understand that it might be a long, hard road if you stay in this marriage?

CHAPTER 8

BUSTED

Human tracking device

What is a GPS? How does it work?

The Global Positioning System (GPS) tells you where you are on Earth. Library of Congress. https://www.loc.gov/everyday-mysteries/technology/item/what-is-gps-how-does-it-work/

Webster defines *trust* as "assured reliance on the character, ability, strength, or truth of someone or something."

Spying and sneaking around on your partner can create disagreement. Nonetheless, many individuals admit that they often do just that! It's crucial to look at the pros and cons that your behavior might cause your relationship.

Investigating your spouse's activities without consent establishes spying or sneaking around.

The present digital world offers vast opportunities to watch your spouse's everyday activities.

Reading emails, viewing text messages and call histories, logging into your spouse's social media accounts, or listening to your spouse's voicemail messages are all spying. Please don't forget the good old-fashioned snooping techniques. You are checking your spouse's pockets. Going through a wallet, mail, or other documents counts as spying. Even reading your spouse's diary or journal is spying. Some individuals venture to such an extreme as to hire a private detective to follow their spouse and report back. Others use GPS attached to their partner's vehicle to know their whereabouts constantly.

The problems with spying can create a big problem. If you are spying, it may signal that your marriage already has some deep-rooted issues.

Remember, your spouse has a right to privacy, just as you do. You will damage your relationship further and lose a lot of trusts when your spouse finds out. Heads up: sooner or later, you'll get discovered spying. And afterward, you'll either need to confess or lie to cover your tracks. Another issue with sneaking around and spying is figuring out how you will manage the data you find. Many individuals set out to check whether their life partner is cheating. Well, imagine a scenario in which your life partner isn't. Then, what harm have you caused the relationship? In that case, you've been the one to deceive.

If you suspect your spouse is unfaithful, you might analyze everything with such a level of doubt that you might think all signs highlight an issue. Nonetheless, some of the things you coincidentally find may have an honest explanation.

Spying can consume your life. You invest your time checking on your spouse. This energy could be better spent working on the relationship and chipping away at being your best spouse.

Examine your reasons for not trusting. Please check your heart.

When you have little to no faith in your partner, looking at your true motivation is vital. Maybe you have been harmed in past relationships and fear being hurt again.

Ask yourself if spying or snooping will stop your spouse from cheating. It's important to remember that your efforts will not help the relationship.

Some people seem to spy to prove their hunch that their spouse is, in fact, faithful. There is usually no end. Instead, people become almost like addicts who constantly need to satisfy their curiosity.

Ask yourself whether the thing you are doing is helping the marriage. Spying won't make you trust if you are battling to believe your spouse. It can make a difference and cause the trust to break further, as your spouse may feel you have betrayed their faithfulness.

There is one exemption where it can check out to spy. However, since your mate authorizes you in this situation, it doesn't even genuinely count as spying. Whenever one individual has been untrustworthy, there can be a period of recapturing trust. This can assist one spouse with seeing that the other can be trusted. So, it should only be utilized in certain conditions and just temporarily.

This reminds me of a story. When my husband and I went through this, we needed accountability partners. I needed to learn to trust again. We discussed accountability and what it would look like in our relationship. There would be no more excuses. We would take responsibility for our actions. We decided that we would be intentional and show that we were invested.

Telling the truth at all costs, sharing everything. Giving the password for cell phones, email, computers, etc.

We would not walk away when we got a call.

We avoided commenting on opposite-sex social media.

Suppose you are repairing the marriage. If you have zero faith in your spouse, you must genuinely seek help. A good marriage is based on trust, regard, and reliability. Assuming your marriage comes up short on attributes, possibly there are a few genuine hidden issues that should be addressed immediately. Building trust takes time, yet it can be lost in a moment. If you have no faith in your spouse, think about getting help. It probably isn't going to get any better all alone. Try not to believe that keeping an eye on your companion will deal with your envy, uneasiness, or doubts.

Communication is fundamental in a relationship, but many do not know how to communicate appropriately. Some women think we are good communicators because we can out-talk a man.

You must be clear and concise to be understood so your partner understands what you are attempting to communicate.

Write down your thoughts before you discuss them to stay focused.

A cheating spouse should voluntarily state their whereabouts. Ask your spouse to tell you their whereabouts if you want to know. Set checkpoints, so we do not give the enemy room. Be patient with them.

No boys' night out until trust has been rebuilt. Be consistent; you have to make a conscious effort.

If you tell your spouse you are coming home at six o'clock, do it.

Because of upcoming innovations, we can see a critical expansion in spying. Remember, the data we get from spying can help in many ways, but are you ready for the facts? It can show the real strength of your marriage. Though you are married, it doesn't mean that you don't have any right to keep your details private. You still have rights. There might be some information that you are withholding. And it would be best if you did not share it until you are ready. If financially possible, take a leave from your job and spend time with your spouse. Take your time and try to explain everything, and speak as the Lord leads you. Do not beat around the bush. If you do, it will out you as a liar. Leave no room for misunderstanding; explain yourself fully.

Have you ever created your own opinions based on assumptions? I know I am guilty of that. One day, my husband went to the store and had a flat while out. I had built up this whole scenario in my head that he was faking it and not going to the store. He intended to be with another woman. I was so upset with him when he arrived home. We can eliminate wrong assumptions. Sometimes, this happens because of poor communication.

I heard someone say that partial information is worse than no information. A big part of the information can be lethal. So, try to get complete details.

Your spouse might have installed a GPS on your device without letting you know. The chain will continue, and it will be deadly for your relationship. You shouldn't hide any information from your spouse. Attempt to be available to that person. Then, you will feel better.

They have a right to know what you are doing and where you are. If you tell them, it will build trust. Remember, it doesn't take much to create confusion. You should prevent it at all costs.

Some of the games couples play use fake online profiles. Getting you drunk and then asking you questions. These games are unethical. Remember to stay focused. You are trying to build a strong bond of trust between you.

You should compromise.

Be sure to ask the right questions and be ready for the answer. Do not ask questions or probe for details that lead to further confusion.

I once heard someone advise a person working on a relationship to think of the work as farming, not hunting; it's a process.

A young lady once told me:

> He gave me all his passwords when we moved in. I didn't need them. However, he insisted. And afterward, he'd begin requesting that I answer messages now

and then since it was stuff he would have instead not managed. So, I guess I resembled his secretary. In any case, I chose to browse his email once he was away on business. I observed a wide range of craigslist hookups. He was attempting to connect with somebody while he was away.

I spoke to him when he returned home, and he had the nerve to say I ought to feel sorry for him since it ended up being a man (just webcam destinations and stuff), so he didn't get laid. Some individuals are unremorseful.

A young man once shared how his fiancée had crossed the line in their relationship.

One day, I approached and shocked her as I strolled in on her, taking naked selfies on her telephone. She attempted to pretend that it was me she was sending them to, which I accepted. She put her telephone on the end table; we began playing. She nodded about an hour later, and I got her iPhone to attempt to charge it.

Suddenly, a picture of another guy's private parts came up on the screen, with a note stating "returning the favor."

So, I did what any hurt person would do. I sent the pictures to my email and went on her PC, in a different room. I printed out 25 duplicates of the main image and continued to tape them around her room. I sent her a message saying "Bye." Then, I blocked her number from my cell phone and left.

Infidelity does not start in the bedroom!

Self-Reflection:

1. Are you battling to believe your spouse?

2. Will spying help you trust?

3. Does investigating your spouse's activities without consent establish spying or sneaking around?

4. Will it damage your relationship further if your spouse
   finds out?

____

____

____

____

5. Ask yourself if spying or snooping will stop your spouse
   from cheating.

____

____

____

____

6. Could this energy be better spent working on the relationship
   and chipping away at being the best spouse you can be?

____

____

____

____

7. Have you thought about getting help?

ON THE ROAD TO RECOVERY

Staying focused

At the end of the recovery stages, you will decide how you want to proceed with your healing.

The Road to Recovery - from thinking that we have lived where God needs us to recognize our inability to live without him.

The path on this road is faith, repentance, and rest in him. *"Take my yoke upon you and learn from me, for I am gentle and humble in heart, and you will find rest for your souls. For my yoke is easy, and my burden is light"* (Matthew 11:29-30 NIV).

This section will discuss what you can expect through the process as it connects with the Seven Stages of Grief, based on my experience.

Even though every story is somewhat unique, there is a process we all seem to follow.

Regardless of anything else, realize that recuperating will require some investment. Show restraint; be thinking to yourself. It's a cycle. But remember that wherever you are is where you ought to be.

SHOCK

If you're reading this, you won't be surprised by the shock and agony that will overwhelm you when disloyalty is uncovered. For me, it was consuming. I was unable to eat, rest, or concentrate. The main thing that made a difference was God!

DENIAL

The more I smothered my resentment, hurt, and dissatisfaction, the more prominent those sentiments became. I once heard someone say, "There are three things that can't be covered up: the sun, the moon, and reality. However, I was not too fond of the idea and needed to permit the pain and anger to run their course.

TO BE THE PERFECT SPOUSE

If I had been a better wife—more grounded, more intelligent, taller, more attractive, more effective, less aggressive...if I had met his "needs"—he wouldn't have ever sought out another woman. Looking back, this is utter, complete nonsense! Since when is anyone responsible for making someone else happy?

I cannot answer for someone else's joy. If we happen to make someone comfortable, then great, but it is not our obligation.

GUILT

I took on the burden of guilt. I sincerely convinced myself that this affair had to be my fault because, somehow, I didn't do enough. He didn't blame me outright, as some betrayers do, but he let it be known that he had been unhappy for a while.

ANGER

This was the most destructive phase for me. The wounds were still very fresh, still very tender to the touch. He stated many times that he wanted to stay married. I liked the marriage in my heart, but I was angry and wanted him to hurt!

DEPRESSION

I battled hard. I had to break this feeling and couldn't rely on my spouse to help me through it.

I often felt sad and anxious. I found myself not wanting to do activities that used to be fun.

I felt irritable and easily frustrated. I had trouble falling asleep and staying asleep, for that matter. I had no appetite. I experienced terrible backaches. I had many difficulties concentrating, remembering details, and making decisions and felt helpless. God was and is the only one that could help me. Depression stayed around for a good year and a half at varying levels.

ACCEPTANCE

Please understand that I will never accept my spouse's infidelity. I only acknowledge that it happened. There's a significant difference in that. Nobody is recommending you like, need, or deserve what happens. Yet, I say again: you need to accept that it happens. Acceptance will help YOU move forward in the healing process.

If no one has ever said sorry to you, I am sorry for what brought you here. I am here to support you.

I remember crying daily for at least the first year. I suggest you do things for yourself. Surround yourself with positive people. Permit yourself to feel anything. Just let everything out. I did vast loads of journaling, which genuinely helped. I would have fits of anxiety in the supermarket and begin hollering...I lay on the floor at home when my body felt frail and temperamental...I just let myself be.

I was so furious at my husband. I went for long strolls in the cool air, which made a difference. I did a morning reflection/ breathing routine which helped tremendously. Hydrate well and take vitamins.

Keep the body sound and rest whenever you can. This will assist with bringing some relief from the preoccupied mind. Whether or not you stay in the marriage is up to you; however, deal with yourself and truly investigate what your better half brings to the table. I hope this helps……

Self-Reflection:

1. Have you convinced yourself that this affair was your fault?

2. Have you permitted yourself to feel everything you are feeling?

3. Have you recognized you cannot accomplish your ability?

4. You cannot do it without God.

5. Have you decided you must let this run its course?

6. Are you smothering resentment, hurt, and dissatisfaction?

CHAPTER 10

PEELER

*Coaching removes the layers to get to the
root of the problem.*

I'm sitting here reminiscing how God was peeling back the layers slowly in our life, one layer at a time. I recall jokingly saying, "By the time this ordeal is over, the rapture will have occurred." The process was taking way too long! The Bible reminds us to *"Be still before the Lord and wait patiently for him"* (Psalms 37:7 NIV). I wanted everything to be good overnight. I did not want to go through the process. I was very impatient. I was not sure if I trusted the process. *Will the people we were working with stick with us? Will they give up on us, as I have on many occasions?*

It was excruciating to be vulnerable and expose myself completely. *Will they think it was my fault? Will they think I'm not good enough for him? Do they think I am just plain crazy?*

Am I staying in this marriage so I don't feel like a failure (doing time)? My mind was flooded with thoughts. I was exhausted. I attempted daily to say affirmations and confessions over my marriage. There's nothing wrong with an excellent motivational saying to encourage yourself.

The Bible says that David was "*greatly distressed, for the people spoke of stoning him because all the people were bitter in soul, each for his sons and daughters. But David strengthened himself in the Lord his God*" (1 Samuel 30:6 ESV). However, we must accept reality and allow God to loosen those layers within us so we can truly bloom. We have to allow God to reveal deeply hidden secrets inside. Be emotionally honest – our culture often views emotion as a weakness. Still, the culture is shifting toward authenticity. Remind yourself of God's goodness and what God has done for you when you feel forgotten by God. I dare you to challenge your internal despair and question those thoughts and feelings.

I was very nervous during our first session with our Counselor. I did not know what to expect. I hoped God would reveal everything about my spouse and that I would not have to talk. Unfortunately, that is not my story. The first question was, "How is everything going?"

I abruptly answered sarcastically, "Everything is great. Can't you see it in my face?" I quickly composed myself and changed my attitude.

The counselor said, "Tell me something about your upbringing." Before I answered, I asked myself, *what does my upbringing do with my marriage?* Wait, hear me out. Does anyone else think these questions have nothing to do with marriage? I realized I have trust issues. I am asking this person for help. I must feel safe and trust the process. I understand now that talking about childhood experiences helps us grieve and process any losses or emotional injuries we suffered as children that can roll over to our adult relationships.

As a child, I was sexually abused. I wasn't straightforward and did not want to talk about it. As we discussed the abuse, I discovered I had trust issues from childhood. I was sexually abused by someone I truly loved and trusted very much. **It was not an isolated incident; it happened for years. I remember it vividly, like it was yesterday.** I started to comprehend the weightiness of the circumstance and was very uncomfortable.

As I went through my teen years, I had these incidental flashbacks where these images would just unexpectedly come into my head and stop as abruptly as they came. I thought it was the devil messing with me and did not realize it was God. He no longer wanted me to suppress those emotions.

About six years passed before I could tell my husband about what happened to me in my childhood. I hid it for a long time since I knew how he would respond. I was lost and had no clue about how to manage it. I was lost, alone, and confused.

The agony of holding those memories back until I had an actual plan to deal with them started affecting my behavior and probably even my personality. I did not realize that my mental health had deteriorated entirely over the years. I began having these very explosive moments when I suddenly became angry at others for minor things. Those turned out to be progressively more broken until, one day, I attempted to speak to my father about what he did.

I started the conversation as any other normal conversation with him. Then I went for the jugular: "So why did you do that to me as a child?'" He downplayed it, so I have always had a problem with people not acknowledging my feelings and trying to play them down.

I can sleep with my conscience clear. I can walk with my head up high. But he will have to look at himself in the mirror every day of his life and live with what he did. I later realized I was suppressing my emotions and had not dealt with them. So, these protective measures spilled over into my marriage.

I know the enemy's plan did not want me to know who I was in God. It took me a long time to talk openly to the counselors at my church, and my first attempts were unsuccessful.I eventually explained everything to the counselor, how I was raped repeatedly for a long time, and my disgust after realizing what had happened to me.

I have to admit that, weirdly enough, I felt like a failure until all those memories surfaced since I could see no reasonable explanation for why I would be depressed. I believed I'd had an incredible youth compared to my friends. As far as I was aware, my parents had given me the best they could, so there was no reasonable explanation for why I should feel so depressed. Forgiveness, building bridges, and destroying walls have freed me; you can also be free.

When I returned home from our meeting with the counselor, everything did not get better overnight, but I admit that it took the focus off of my husband and placed it on me. You see, I did not want just to exist. I wanted to live freely and enjoy my life, not merely survive while "doing time." I found myself fighting yet another demon.

After so long, I am pleased to say I have continued, and he no longer overwhelms my thoughts. I have come to acknowledge that I am the individual I am; the essence of me is simply the result of the combination of all experiences I went through in my life; the good and the bad, the best and, indeed, the ugly.

So as much as I would have preferred not to have been sexually abused, the reality was that I was. And as much as that influences the person I am today, what truly makes me who I am is what I decided to do with it and the type of person I would become due to it. In other words, I would not become the kind of person I would become because of it but who I would become despite it. However, with time, growth, and, without a doubt, spending time in God's presence, I understood one specific thing: I needed to forgive.

Our misery turned into our ministry. I am so happy to say that we have been happily married for thirty years. I want to emphasize that we are *happily* married, not just "doing time." I am more accessible than I have ever been in my life. Life is not perfect, but we serve a perfect God, and if we acknowledge him in all our ways, he will lead us.

We have a ministry called Mission Possible Marriage Ministry. Mission Possible understands the needs of couples struggling in their marriage. We are prepared to coach one-on-one with couples in a private, face-to-face, or virtual environment. You and your spouse will be ready to deal with struggles, develop communication, build intimacy, and restore your marriage.

Are you married and miserable (*doing time*) just to say you are married, or are you ready to take your marriage to the next level? I was a prisoner. You cannot continue living your life trying to protect others, children, or the church. You also can be free. I'm a prisoner no longer!

Consider working with us. We will help you uncover, value, and share it authentically. Let's go!

THE LETTERS

Try to read from a place of understanding and empathy. People need to define their goals, needs, and vision for their relationship in the beginning stages of a relationship. Speaking up for yourself is taking care of yourself.

To help with the healing process, you should understand that you matter. You have a voice, and that voice should be heard.

Many individuals are reluctant to speak up for themselves or support themselves because of a paranoid fear of rejection. Truthfully, just because you use your voice doesn't mean you're assured of the results you are looking for or need. Your accomplice is still entitled to express their needs as well.

This is significant because, occasionally, it is difficult to utilize your voice. You need to keep silent and allow others to represent you. Whenever you do this, you lose part of your identity. Having a voice implies being able to overcome the world. Your voice counts!

Letter from husband to wife

Dear wife,

I'm so ashamed of myself right now.

My heart is hurting, and my hands are shaking as I'm writing this, as I search my heart to express how awful I feel about myself.

I deeply regret the pain I have caused you and the kids. I honestly regret my actions. I secretly pray and wish that the hands of the clock could be turned back so it could never have happened. Remember how we met and went through thick and thin up to this moment? We've come a long way, babe, and I wouldn't give or trade anything for you. You're all I've got. Please forgive me.

I take full responsibility for my actions and would never pretend like it never happened. Please find a place in your heart to forgive me and give me another chance to make things right. I'm in so much pain now, and I wish you could see it. I have not only disappointed the woman I loved and still love but caused her pain and emotional trauma. I see your pain. I see you toss and turn in our bed every night. I regret every sleepless night I have caused.

Please don't let anything come between us. I will never give another woman any room to come close to me again. I have cut ties with her, and she's now in the past. I have also realized that I was too selfish, which affected my thinking, judgment, and emotions. Now I know better.

I've vowed to be a better man for you and the kids. I don't want to tell you that I'm a changed man now, but I want you to see that I've changed. You've got every right to be mad at me, that's okay, and I won't blame you for any action you may want to take. But I beg you, please forgive me. I pray for God to heal you every day. I know I've hurt you badly but allow me to prove myself.

Honestly, words are just not doing justice to how I feel inside. All the same, I'll keep trying, hoping you can see through to my soul and have mercy on me. I've got you and the kids, and I can't afford to lose my family.

I love you with every fiber of my being, and I am willing to do anything so we can heal from this trauma I have caused. Please forgive me. I'm sorry for what happened, and I promise you, darling, it will never happen again.

Regards,

Signed The unfaithful husband

Letter from the mistress to the wife

I thought about writing to you often. Whenever I pick up my pen, I question if I should do it. If so, what do I even say? How can I put into words the emotions that consume me? Every day, the regret I feel overwhelms every aspect of my life.

There is no excuse for the wrongdoings Tony and I have committed. The worst kind of betrayal, one I never wanted to be a part of. I understand just how hurtful and soul-crushing our actions are. I never intended to hurt you or your family. I am not that person. I never wanted to put anyone in the position I've put you in. I never wanted to be that girl.

I know you may not want to hear what I have to say. I understand. I get it. You don't owe me the time to read this letter. However, I want to express the weight these decisions have carried.

The guilt consumes me every moment. It never wavers or subsidies. I struggle to eat, sleep, and work. I have asked myself why I made the decisions – I cannot give you an answer. I wish I could, but I am even shocked at my actions. I am disappointed that I've caused the most profound pain – a pain I once felt in a previous relationship. I can only express my sincerest, most profound apology.

They say no one is perfect, and everyone makes mistakes. I know that to be true, and yes – I've made my share of bad decisions. But this one is the one I regret the most. If I could change our history and remove all contact, I would do it in a heartbeat. Unfortunately, this isn't an option.

While I cannot give you a why I can only offer my apology, I hope you can find it in your heart to forgive us for our actions. If not for us, for yourself. You deserve to find peace and happiness after all you've been through. I know it has been a challenging journey that I'll regret. I hope you can find love for life again one day, to wake up without pain tormenting your heart.

Regarding Tony, I have cut all ties with him and promise never to contact him again. Out of respect for your family, I will not get in the way of any of your future growth and healing. This will be the only letter. I just wanted you to know just how awful I feel. I wanted you to know that I am genuinely sorry for everything and wish so badly that it never happened.

I take full responsibility for what transpired between Tony and me. It was wrong, and I knew it was. I should not have pursued him or entertained the idea of being with him. I honestly don't know what I was thinking. I know I have learned from this and never want to do this again – with anyone. Forever sorry.

Signed the mistress

Letter from The Wife to the mistress

Hello Miss, or should I say, Mistress:

I don't know much about you and prefer to keep it that way. All I have is an address, and he said he'll never again be at your door. My husband wouldn't even utter your name. I see you as a damaged silhouette of a woman, a nameless lady waiting in the shadows. I am using the word *lady* loosely. I don't want to give you that much respect, especially since you didn't have an ounce of care for me. No compassion, no sympathy... Where is your empathy?

Could you imagine if this all was done to you? I am strong, so when you realize the devastation and destruction you have caused, I will refuse to bear your grief, and I surely don't need your pity. It's pretty sad. You are just sorry, a fool who shared a defiled bed with a bigger fool. Karma will catch up to you, and it won't house any good.

My mind wandered for many days about what was happening with my husband. I had many restless nights attempting to figure out what was wrong. I couldn't fully function, and the thoughts took their toll. I fell into despair and succumbed to the weight of loneliness; I squirmed in a bed alone. He assured me he was mandated to work overtime. He had no free time, it seemed. I felt ungrateful that this man was working so hard, but all I could do was look side-eye with doubt. My family kept reminding me of what a great man I have, and there was no need to worry.

I know he is in ministry and claimed he was devoted to meeting that schedule. He reminded me that I was his first ministry, and we would spend quality time together soon. I could hear the falsetto of Eddie Kendricks echo in the back of my mind, "It was just my imagination; once again, running away with me." The reality of it all is that he was keeping you warm. He went from the church house to the whore's house.

You must have been taught, "Having a man, any man, is better than not having a man at all." This was probably learned behavior. Your mother must've been the *other woman with the family* who lived on the town's less beautified side. That back patio door would creak open every few weeks, letting you know your dad was coming by for a brief moment. You probably were so happy, and you thought that type of life was standard. You carried that Jezebel spirit, a generational curse indeed. You probably met my husband at the church. You went in there as a visitor, walking in with oily legs, no stockings, sitting in the front with a short skirt, looking for attention. I've seen your type a dozen times. You aren't unique, just commonly plain. Too bad common sense wasn't present to help prevent this madness from occurring. Once upon a time, I was proud to say, "That's my husband." We were so happy and built a great life together. Now I am so embarrassed and ashamed.

You are a homewrecker. He may have lusted after you, but I am the one he's in love with. No matter how hard you try, you could never be me. If he can't appreciate my passion and how I have always been there, it's his loss. I was praying for him and with him. How could he do this to me? When his family dogged him out, I was there to uplift him. There was a time he was struggling, and I helped support his dreams. I cooked, cleaned, and made sure I was a good wife. I know who I am. Our sex life was amazing. It takes years to know someone completely. I did a bid, putting all that time in. I didn't learn everything about him as I thought I did. Was this some cruel life sentence? Talk about "until death does us part." What a joke!

All these years were wasted. I made so many sacrifices and never complained. I carried his babies; I am the mother of his children. Now, he comes to me begging like he received a revelation. Instead of being laid up, you and he both need to lay on the altar. You can't get away with this. God sees you and knows all things. You and my funny-looking husband both need to repent and seek deliverance. I pray to our Heavenly Father that the conviction is on your soulless heart. You have the nerve to be somebody's mistress. I thought he and I had something special. I see it couldn't have been, or none of this would have happened.

I can't believe I cried over him. Felt sick to my stomach because of the deceit. I was betrayed by the very person who vowed to love me. Life can be one big joke. The pain was unbearable. After all this, a man appears not to be worth one tear. My husband said he wants his family. Please believe he will never leave me. I don't even want him at this point, but he can bring that check home to me. Miss, whatever your name is, I wish you well. I hope this letter finds you in hell, where you deserve to be.

Signed, a too-outdone wife
about to live her best—not bitter—life.

[Published] Contributor: Q.R. Williams

Letter from the mistress to the wife

Hello,

You don't know me, and quite frankly, I almost feel embarrassed to say that I know your husband. I guess you can say I'm his mistress. I know that no woman wants to find out like this. I want to say I'm sorry, but the reality is that if I were sorry, I would have never become involved with him. When I first met him, I had no intention of anything happening between us. I've never dated a married man or a man who was in a situation. We worked for the same company and were introduced through a mutual colleague.

We began working on a project together and completed that project. It was all platonic. There was a new project, and he called me to work on it with him and his team. We first went wrong because we exchanged phone numbers, but it was supposed to be strictly business. At work, we formed a united front and a friendship. I realize now that this was the start of an emotional attachment. We started working late hours together, which is how we slowly developed feelings. I was a hurt woman who had my fair share of disappointments, and well, sorry to say, I later found out that he was unhappy. I did not know that initially. He never let on that there were issues between you, which was a turn-on. Our calls went from business to sharing things about our lives. I was so busy pouring out my hurt, and he would just listen and offer advice. We began to lean on each other for everything. It got to the point where the feelings were obvious between us. Initially, it was all energy with no intimacy, and we both tried to keep it from each other, but we were falling for each other…

I know you don't want to hear this, but you and I share some things. We are both women who share the same man. We both desire to be in a monogamous relationship with a good man. I believe that we both have a good man, though! I see how he looks at me, and I know he appreciates the comfort I provide, but I can also see how he knows what he is doing is wrong. I like that. He has a conscience, yes. I can also see that he loves you. Knowing that he loves you does hurt me, but the love he provides to me sustains me as well. We also share the hurt that he loves another woman. If I could offer you one thing, it would be this: please learn how to treat him, clean the house, cook for him, and raise your kids with love. You are unfriendly, and you must keep yourself clean and well-groomed. He needs support and respect. You are the opposite of these things, so now I am filling in and want to win.

I like your man! I want to give him what he deserves! I am here to listen and allow him to bear his soul and get everything you refuse to give him from me. I know, I know, I know. I have a lot of nerve, and yes, he is wrong for sharing his frustrations with me, but you refuse to listen. I know I shouldn't be the one to tell you why to listen to me, but you have a man who would never go outside his marriage if you just did the bare minimum. You practically pushed him into my arms! I am his friend, confidant, advisor, lover, and biggest fan. Come on; I am giving you hints. When you hurt him with your words, I lift him with my words. When you scream and curse him, I speak love and blessings.

When you don't support him, I scream his name loud! I am everything you're not, and I can't help that! I can see the king he'll become while you tell him he isn't! While you shoot down his vision, I am here to execute it. Why am I in this space? Maybe he won't need me anymore if you heed the hints. One day, I would like to say that I'll stop being with your husband, but I am so tied to him now. So, I'll say what I feel, and that is, I hope you continue to mess up, so in the end, I win. I know you share many things, but I don't even want those things. I want his heart.

Signed The Mistress

A letter from the wife to the husband

There was a stranger in our bed last night. I know you're reading this wondering what I'm talking about. Where were you? What is happening right now?

I'll explain as best as I can.

Last night I came to bed to find a man there that I thought I knew. He smelled like you. His silhouette in the dark was almost identical to the man I married. He called me by my name. I surrendered into his arms, believing it was you. As I smelled him and held him, it was you. I wasn't confused. I know my husband. Or I thought I did.

As the events unfolded, I noticed differences between this man and the

man I've known for almost twenty years. The voice was different. It was cold and demanding. Not the warm, caressing whisper that I've heard time and time again. Even his movements were inexplicably strange. He was fierce and calculated, as if he had something to prove. Was he trying to prove something to himself or me?

I'm not sure I know. The passion wasn't there. It was strange and unfamiliar. He didn't surrender into my arms. You weren't there. I tried to look into his eyes, but he couldn't face me.

Even in the dark, I could see his eyes were focused anywhere but my face. I missed that deep, longing look into my eyes as you softly whispered my name. Instead, there were phrases. Phrases in English you had never spoken.

Phrases you'd never speak to your wife. You've never spoken out of our native tongue in the bedroom, yet here you were. I felt so lost and so confused.

Who was this man that resembled you but was nothing like you? Why was he in my bed?

The night mechanically unfolded with me in a sad state of confusion. I couldn't understand what was happening or why. I didn't know how to ask you. Maybe this was all in my head? Perhaps I was just not used to change or something new?

But no, as you lay next to me with your eyes focused on the ceiling above me, I realized it wasn't you. Even your breathing was noticeably different.

I said goodnight, but you didn't answer. You were busy replying to what I assumed was a text from work. But as I drifted off to sleep, the reality of that night rushed over me like a complex wave. You weren't the different one. It was my husband in our bed. He just wasn't in bed with me. It was another woman who entered our intimacy. I just didn't see her walk in.

Sign the Wife

Letter of forgiveness

With this letter, I am choosing to forgive you.

I accept what happened and am ready to let go of my resentment. I don't want to be angry anymore. I release it!

When I found out what you did, it broke my heart into a million pieces. I was so shocked and confused, but it was the betrayal that hurt the most. It felt like everything we'd gone through together was suddenly meaningless, and it left a huge empty hole in my life. I felt like I'd given you so much of myself. I didn't know how to move on or trust again for a time. The hurt was so deep. I harbored a lot of anger for too long.

I hadn't realized you were unhappy in our relationship. Looking back, I don't think you did it in malice. Maybe boredom and excitement of a new experience. You were tempted by lust and made a wrong decision. I disapprove of what you did, yet we've all made mistakes.

I'm thankful for the love you showed me for a period. I'm likewise grateful that I learned I can't characterize my value by what a man finds in me. While it required investment, I've acquired strength in getting through this experience.

I let go of the past and its control over me.

Dear Lord, I thank You for the power of forgiveness, and I choose to forgive everyone who has hurt me. Help me set [name anyone who has offended you] free and release them to You. *"Do not take revenge, my dear friends, but leave room for God's wrath, for it is written: 'It is mine to avenge; I will repay,' says the Lord"* (Romans 12:19 NIV).

Remember That This Is for You, Not the One Who Hurt You

Myths About Forgiveness
- Forgiving someone automatically means you think they shouldn't be punished
- Forgiveness makes you weak
- Forgiveness means you forget about the offending act
- Forgiveness requires reconciliation (restoring friendly relations) with the offender

Forgiveness is, therefore, a powerful method of:
- Stress relief
- Lowered risk of heart attack
- Improved cholesterol
- Better sleep
- Reduced pain
- Lowered blood pressure
- Improvements in anxiety and depression
- Strengthened immune system
- Improved self-esteem

Just think about it; until you forgive someone, you're harboring festering anger and resentment. Having those feelings bottled up inside creates chronic stress, which is toxic to your body, psychologically and physically.

Set aside a block of time when you won't be interrupted, put on gentle music that inspires you, light some candles, and set all your intentions toward forgiveness and release.

As mentioned earlier, it's important to remember that this forgiveness isn't about absolving the other person (or people) of all the horrible things they did to you.

Let this act of forgiveness sever all cords and close all doors to them forever.

Still need some help on your healing journey? Talking with somebody can assist you with taking care of anything life tosses at you. It's a great way to get your thoughts and worries out of your head so you can work through them. I recommend you speak to a therapist rather than a friend or relative since they are professionally trained.

While you might attempt to manage this yourself, it could be a more critical issue than self-improvement can address. Forgiveness takes strength and practice. Saying "I forgive you" alone isn't enough. There has to be a fundamental change on the inside.

98

GLOSSARY

https://www.insideprison.com/glossary.asp

Prison Slang | Terms, Meanings & Popular Phrases

Slang words I used in each chapter:

Busted - slang for when a person gets caught in a lie

Midnight Express (run) - prison slang for an old-fashioned escape attempt

Control Center Ministers - Control Units are sections of a maximum-security facility. Most fully characterize the notion of deterrence for the most dangerous and criminally-minded offenders in the prison system. The booth's vantage point allows the constant observation of all cells through security cameras and sound systems. Prisoners are confined to their cells for 23 hours a day and are allowed 1 hour of exercise in a tightly guarded and controlled exercise yard.

Potting - prison slang for throwing or dumping a bucket of excrement on a correctional officer

Prison guards/officers/Chota (ministers) - correctional officer, someone who guards prisoners.

Keeper - someone in charge of other people, as in, "Am I my brother's keeper?"

Psychopath (abnormal behavior) - someone who is suffering from psychopathy. Psychopathy is a classifiable personality.

Not a scooby - I don't have a clue. No idea.

Pass system (GPS) - a program similar to a temporary absence, where inmates are allowed to leave prison, with a correctional staff escort, for humanitarian, health, rehabilitative, or medical reasons. Frequent leaves are granted for family visits, education and employment opportunities, and recreational activities such as sports events.

On the road to recovery - slang for being finally out of prison

Peeler - slang for police or cops (used in this book for counselor/coach)

Social media tags

- https://www.facebook.com/missionpossiblemarriageministry

- https://www.linkedin.com/in/merihorton

- https://www.instagram.com/merihorton/

- https://twitter.com/boricuahorton

- Website https://missionpossibleinstitute.com/

- YouTube: https://www.youtube.com/channel/UChnWt0b4lIl71tJI2yZwPIQ